S0-DFD-665

David
and Goliath

Cover illustration by
Michael Jaroszko

Story adaptation by
Sarah Toast

Interior illustrations by
Thomas Gianni

Interior art consultation by
David M. Howard, Jr., Ph.D.

Copyright © 1995 Publications International, Ltd.
All rights reserved. This book may not be reproduced or quoted in whole or in part by mimeograph or any other printed or electronic means, or for presentation on radio, television, videotape, or film without written permission from

Louis Weber, C.E.O.
Publications International, Ltd.
7373 North Cicero Avenue
Lincolnwood, Illinois 60646

Permission is never granted for commercial purposes.

Manufactured in U.S.A.

8 7 6 5 4 3 2 1

ISBN: 0-7853-1156-4

PUBLICATIONS INTERNATIONAL, LTD.
Little Rainbow is a trademark of Publications International, Ltd.

Long ago in Bethlehem, there lived a shepherd boy named David. He was the youngest of Jesse's eight handsome and strong sons.

God had looked into David's heart and found him to be a very good person. He chose the boy to be the king of Israel someday. The spirit of God watched over David through many years of hardship before he became king.

For now, David worked hard to take care of his father's sheep. Every day he took his staff, his sling, and his harp and went off to tend the sheep.

Saul was the king of Israel at that time. He was a very unhappy man.

One day when Saul was especially sad, a servant said that harp music might make him feel better. Saul agreed. "Find someone who plays the harp well, and bring him to me," he said.

Another servant had heard that a son of Jesse played the harp very well. So Saul sent a message to Jesse, asking him to send his son David to court.

Jesse loaded a donkey with gifts for Saul and delivered them with David to Saul's court.

David's music made Saul feel much better, so Saul asked Jesse to let David stay at the palace to serve him. David went back and forth from Saul's court to Bethlehem, where he still tended to his father's sheep.

Meanwhile, Saul's army was getting ready to fight the Philistines. The three oldest of David's brothers were in Saul's army. Jesse asked David to take food to them and bring back any news.

David got up early the next day to take the food for his brothers to where the army was camped.

David came to the camp as the armies were lining up for battle. He left the food with a guard and ran quickly to greet his brothers.

As David stood with his brothers, the huge Philistine giant, Goliath, came forward and shouted, "Today I dare Israel to send a man to fight me! If he kills me, then we will be your servants. But if I kill him, then the Israelites must serve the Philistines!"

Saul's soldiers were very frightened and ran from Goliath. But David spoke up, "I will go and fight this Philistine!"

David's brothers were all very fearful. They wanted him to go back home and watch the sheep. But someone had told King Saul what David had said.

Saul sent for David and said to him, "You can't fight this giant. You are just a boy, and he is a warrior."

David responded, "But I have killed both lions and bears to protect the sheep. This giant has challenged the army of the living God. Just as God has saved me from the lions and bears when I was protecting the sheep, He will save me from Goliath."

Saul believed David and allowed him to battle the giant. He said, "Go, and may the Lord be with you."

King Saul gave David his armor to wear—a coat of mail, a bronze helmet, and even his sword. David had never worn heavy armor, and he could barely walk in it.

David took off Saul's armor. And he grabbed his staff and went to pick out five smooth stones from the edge of the stream. These he put in his pouch next to his sling. Then David walked calmly toward Goliath.

Goliath, huge and strong, was covered with armor. He wore a helmet on his head, and his body was covered with a heavy coat of armor. There was also armor strapped to both his legs, and he carried a heavy spear and a sword.

When Goliath saw the unarmed boy coming toward him, he became furious. Goliath snarled loudly, "Am I a dog, that you come to fight me with only a stick?" The giant then cursed and threatened David. "If you come near me, you will end up as food for the wild animals!" Goliath said.

David responded to the menacing giant, "You come at me with sword and spear, but I come here in the name of the Lord. The Lord of Israel's army is stronger than any warrior. And God will help me strike you down so that all people will know how great He is."

When Goliath started moving toward David to fight, the boy ran quickly toward the battle line to meet him. David thrust his hand in his pouch, took out a stone, and put it in his sling. David whirled the sling around his head and quickly let the stone fly.

The stone flew from David's sling, and it struck Goliath's forehead. With a look of pained surprise, the giant fell face down on the ground.

David quickly ran and stood over the stricken giant. Then he pulled Goliath's sword out of its sheath. David killed the giant warrior with his own huge sword.

The Philistines ran when they saw that their best warrior was dead. Saul's army gave a great shout and chased the Philistines a long way. When they came back, they took what they wanted from the tents the Philistines had left behind.

Saul was very grateful to David and asked him to live as a royal son.

David did well wherever Saul sent him, so Saul made David the leader of the army. He won many more battles against the Philistines.

David continued to play his harp. He later became a beloved king of Israel.

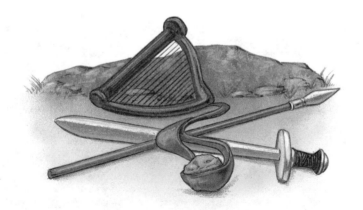